Geography Zone: Landforms™

Exploring
CAVES

Melody S. Mis

PowerKiDS press.

New York

To Laura Howard and her son, Joe

Published in 2009 by The Rosen Publishing Group, Inc.
29 East 21st Street, New York, NY 10010

First Edition

Editor: Nicole Pristash
Book Design: Julio Gil
Photo Researcher: Jessica Gerweck

Photo Credits: Cover, pp. 5, 7, 9, 17 Shutterstock.com; p. 11 © www.iStockphoto.com/Asbjorn Aakjaer; p. 13 © Jerry Dodrill/Getty Images; p. 15 © ARCO/Therin-Weise/AgeFotostock; p. 19 © John R. MacGregor/Peter Arnold Inc.; p. 21 © www.iStockphoto.com/Yewen Lu.

Library of Congress Cataloging-in-Publication Data

Mis, Melody S.
    Exploring caves / Melody S. Mis. — 1st ed.
        p. cm. — (Geography zone. Landforms)
    Includes index.
    ISBN 978-1-4358-2713-4 (library binding) — ISBN 978-1-4358-3111-7 (pbk.)
ISBN 978-1-4358-3117-9 (6-pack)
    1. Caves—Juvenile literature. 2. Cave ecology—Juvenile literature. I. Title.
    GB601.2.M57 2009
    551.44'7—dc22
                                                            2008025753

Manufactured in the United States of America

Contents

What Is a Cave?

A cave is a large, **enclosed** space inside Earth that has an opening to the **surface**. Caves are found in many places. They can be found in mountains, rocky cliffs, and inside ice. There may even be a cave near your house!

You can find cool things inside caves. Many caves have weird shapes along the walls and on the floor. You can also find lots of animals and plants in caves.

Do you want to know more? Let's take a look at how caves are formed and **explore** some of the most interesting caves around.

Caves are found in different parts of the world.
This cave is on South Island, in New Zealand.

5

Caves are some of nature's most common landforms. This is because caves are formed by natural actions that happen every day. Many caves are made when water drips on rocks over and over again. Sea caves are made when ocean waves pound against a rocky shore. **Lava** and melting ice form other types of caves.

Caves can take **millions** of years to take shape. In fact, Jenolan Caves, in Australia, are some of the oldest caves on Earth. They took around 340 million years to form. Like Jenolan Caves, many of the oldest caves in the world are formed in rock.

Here you can see waves forming several sea caves. The waves are slowly wearing away the rock by crashing against it over and over again.

The most common type of cave is a solutional cave. This type of cave is generally made in limestone. Limestone is a soft rock that covers much of Earth. Limestone caves are made when underground water eats through limestone and **carves** out holes. Over time, these holes get bigger. Sometimes, the holes get so big that they become caves.

When water drips through the limestone, the water forms interesting shapes, called stalactites and stalagmites. Stalactites hang from the top of the cave. Stalagmites build up from the bottom. Stalactites and stalagmites often look like soda straws or short trees!

These are stalactites and stalagmites inside a solutional cave. Stalactites and stalagmites are very fragile. This means that they can break easily.

Caves can also form inside ice. These caves are called glacier caves. Glaciers are very large sheets of ice. They are found toward the tops of high mountains and in very cold places, such as the Arctic and Antarctica. Glacier caves form when ice melts. As the ice melts, it forms large holes inside the glaciers. Sometimes, the holes grow bigger and become caves.

Some people mix ice caves up with glacier caves. Ice caves do not form in glaciers. Instead, ice caves are limestone caves or sea caves that have ice inside them that never melts.

This is a glacier cave in Rhône Glacier. Rhne Glacier supplies water to the Rhône River, which runs through Switzerland and France.

A sea cave is another type of cave. Sea caves are formed when strong winds cause ocean waves to beat against rocks on the shore. This causes pieces of the rock to **erode**. After many years, a hole forms where the rock has eroded. This hole becomes a sea cave as it grows bigger.

The longest sea cave in the world is Painted Cave on Santa Cruz Island, in California. Painted Cave is almost ¼ mile (402 m) long and 100 feet (30 m) wide. It is named Painted Cave because of its many bright and colorful rocks.

This is a sea cave on the coast of California. Some of the largest sea caves in the world are found in California and in Hawaii.

Volcanoes form caves as well. When a volcano **erupts**, lava runs down the mountainside and forms a tube, or tunnel, in the ground. The lava on top of the tube gets hard as the lava inside the tube stays soft. When the soft lava flows out of the tube, it leaves a hole. The hole then becomes a lava tube cave.

Fracture caves are caused by rocks falling away from one another. Soft rocks often lie in between hard rocks. If the soft rocks erode, they fall away and leave a hole. As the hole gets bigger, it becomes a cave.

The Galápagos Islands, in South America, are volcanic islands. The volcanoes' eruptions have made many lava tube caves there, like this one.

Even though caves often look dark and empty, there is a lot of life inside them. Animals and plants live in caves, just as they do on other landforms. Animals use caves for many things. Snakes, lizards, and mice hunt for food in caves. Bugs, worms, and spiders spend time in them, too. Bears **hibernate** in caves during the long winter months.

Plants that do not need a lot of sunlight, such as mosses, grow very well in rocky caves. Cave plants grow mostly near the cave's opening, where there is some light to help them stay alive.

Many bats, such as this eastern pipistrelle, spend their days inside caves. They are nocturnal, which means they hunt and feed only at night.

Mammoth Cave, in Kentucky, is known for its **blind** fish. They live in water inside the cave. These fish do not have eyes, but they have **adapted** to the dark. They can feel when other fish are near them in the water even though they cannot see them!

Mammoth Cave is part of a system. A cave system is a group of caves joined together by pathways. The Mammoth Cave system is around 365 miles (587 km) long and has more than 200 caves in it. This makes it one of the largest cave systems in the world.

This blind crayfish has adapted to living in the dark waters of Mammoth Cave. Animals that live in total darkness are called troglobites.

New Mexico has a large cave system called Carlsbad Caverns. "Cavern" is another word for a large cave. Carlsbad is made up of more than 100 caves with colorful rocks in different shapes. These caverns were formed when **acid** dripped through the limestone and formed large holes in the rock.

Bats are the most famous animals of Carlsbad Caverns. Thousands of them live in the Bat Cave. Every evening, the bats fly out of the cave all at once. They look like a giant black cloud in the sky! Many people visit Carlsbad just to see this sight.

The Big Room of Carlsbad Caverns, shown here, covers between 8 and 12 acres (3–5 ha). It is the biggest cave in Carlsbad Caverns.

People like to explore caves for fun. This is called caving or spelunking. There are also people who study and work in caves. These people study the many types of rocks, plants, and animals that are found inside them.

You can explore caves on your own. Maybe you will go with your family or on a school trip. Walking around caves is fun. You can learn a lot by looking at the walls and seeing the strange shapes inside them. If you do visit a cave, be safe, and remember that you are inside one of the world's coolest landforms!

Glossary

acid (A-sud) Something that breaks down matter faster than water does.

adapted (uh-DAPT-ed) Changed to fit requirements.

blind (BLYND) Cannot use the sense of sight.

carves (KAHRVZ) Cuts into a shape.

enclosed (in-KLOHZD) Having something on all sides.

erode (ih-ROHD) To be worn away slowly.

erupts (ih-RUPTS) Breaks open.

explore (ek-SPLOR) To go over carefully.

hibernate (HY-bur-nayt) To spend the winter in a sleeplike state.

lava (LAH-vuh) Hot, melted rock that comes out of a volcano.

millions (MIL-yunz) Very large numbers.

surface (SER-fes) The outside of anything.

volcanoes (vol-KAY-nohz) Openings that sometimes shoot up lava.

Index

A
Antarctica, 10
Arctic, 10
Australia, 6

B
bats, 20
bears, 16

C
California, 12
Carlsbad Caverns, 20

G
glaciers, 10

J
Jenolan Caves, 6

L
limestone, 8, 10

M
Mammoth Cave, 18
mosses, 16

N
New Mexico, 20

P
Painted Cave, 12

S
stalactites, 8
stalagmites, 8

V
volcanoes, 14

Web Sites

Due to the changing nature of Internet links, PowerKids Press has developed an online list of Web sites related to the subject of this book. This site is updated regularly. Please use this link to access the list:
www.powerkidslinks.com/gzone/cave/